GREAT QUOTES FROM GREAT WOMEN

INSPIRATION, MOTIVATION, AND EMPOWERMENT FROM HISTORY'S MOST SUCCESSFUL WOMEN

VOLUME 1

© Copyright 2023 Veronica Jones

All rights reserved.

I created this anthology to celebrate the strength, resilience, and wisdom of women who have made a difference in the world.

Through the words of these remarkable women, my hope is to inspire and empower you to face challenges head-on and embrace your unique journey.

May these timeless quotes serve as a guiding light, instilling courage and confidence in the hearts of women everywhere.

Veronica Jones

LAUREL THATCHER ULRICH

Well-behaved women seldom make history.

MAYA ANGELOU

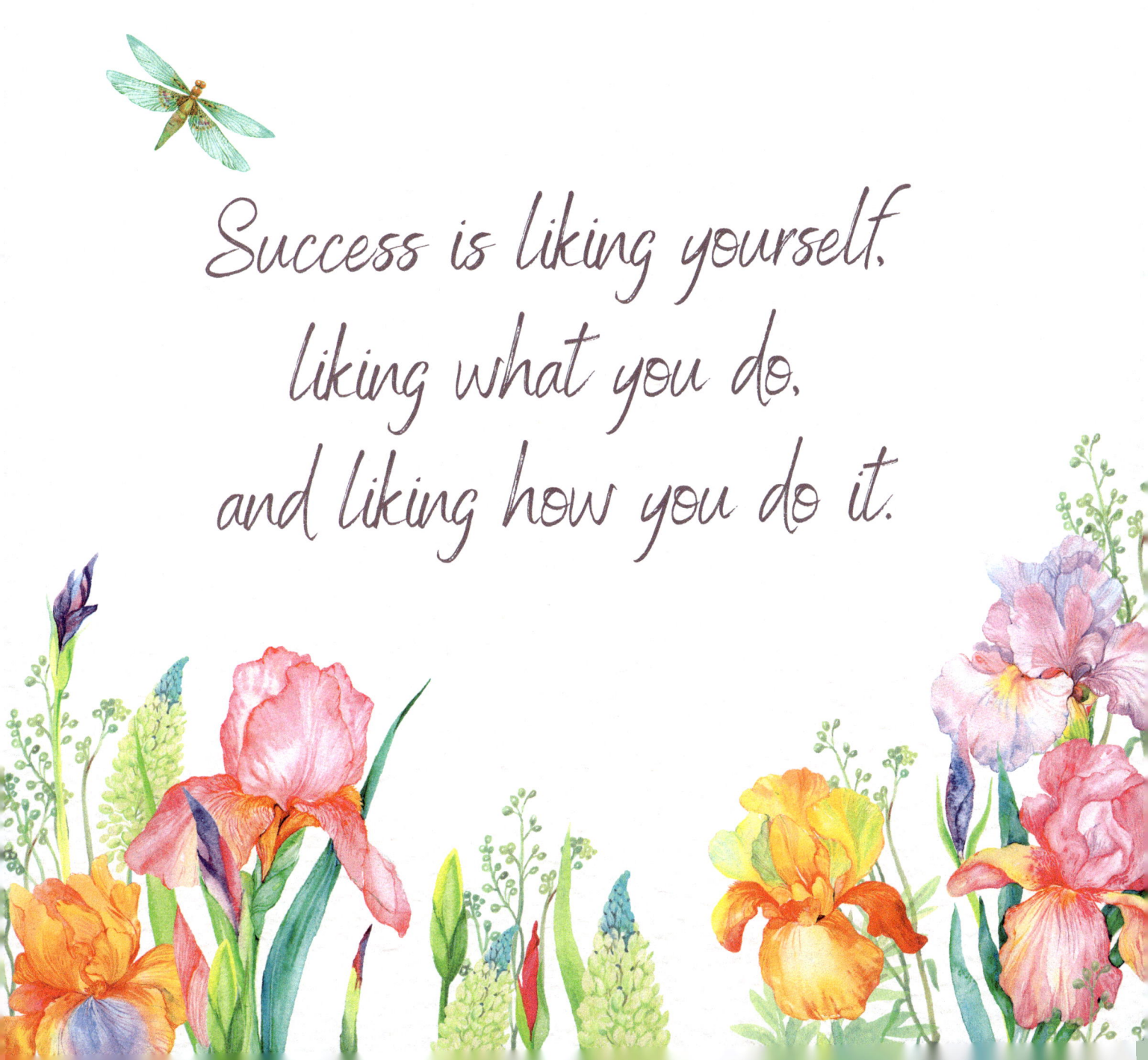

*Success is liking yourself,
liking what you do,
and liking how you do it.*

KATHARINE HEPBURN

If you obey all the rules, you miss all the fun.

ELEANOR ROOSEVELT

No one can make you feel inferior without your consent.

DOLLY PARTON

If you don't like the road you're walking, start paving another one.

COCO CHANEL

The most courageous act is still to think for yourself. Aloud.

AMELIA EARHART

Adventure is worthwhile in itself.

SHERYL SANDBERG

In the future, there will be no female leaders. There will just be leaders.

MELISSA ETHERIDGE

You are more powerful than you know; you are beautiful just as you are.

SARA BLAKELY

Don't be intimidated by what you don't know. That can be your greatest strength.

EMMA STONE

I can't think of any better representation of beauty than someone who is unafraid to be herself.

BETHANY HAMILTON

Courage, sacrifice, determination, commitment, toughness, heart, talent, guts. That's what little girls are made of.

MALALA YOUSAFZAI

Do not wait for someone else to come and speak for you. It's you who can change the world.

MAYA ANGELOU

I am a woman phenomenally. Phenomenal woman, that's me.

YOKO ONO

You change the world
by being yourself.

HELEN KELLER

Optimism is the faith that leads to achievement.

ANONYMOUS

A strong woman stands up for herself. A stronger woman stands up for everyone else.

VIRGINIA WOOLF

For most of history, Anonymous was a woman.

ANNE FRANK

How wonderful it is that nobody need wait a single moment before starting to improve the world.

GABBY DOUGLAS

Don't be afraid to speak up for yourself. Keep fighting for your dreams!

MAYA ANGELOU

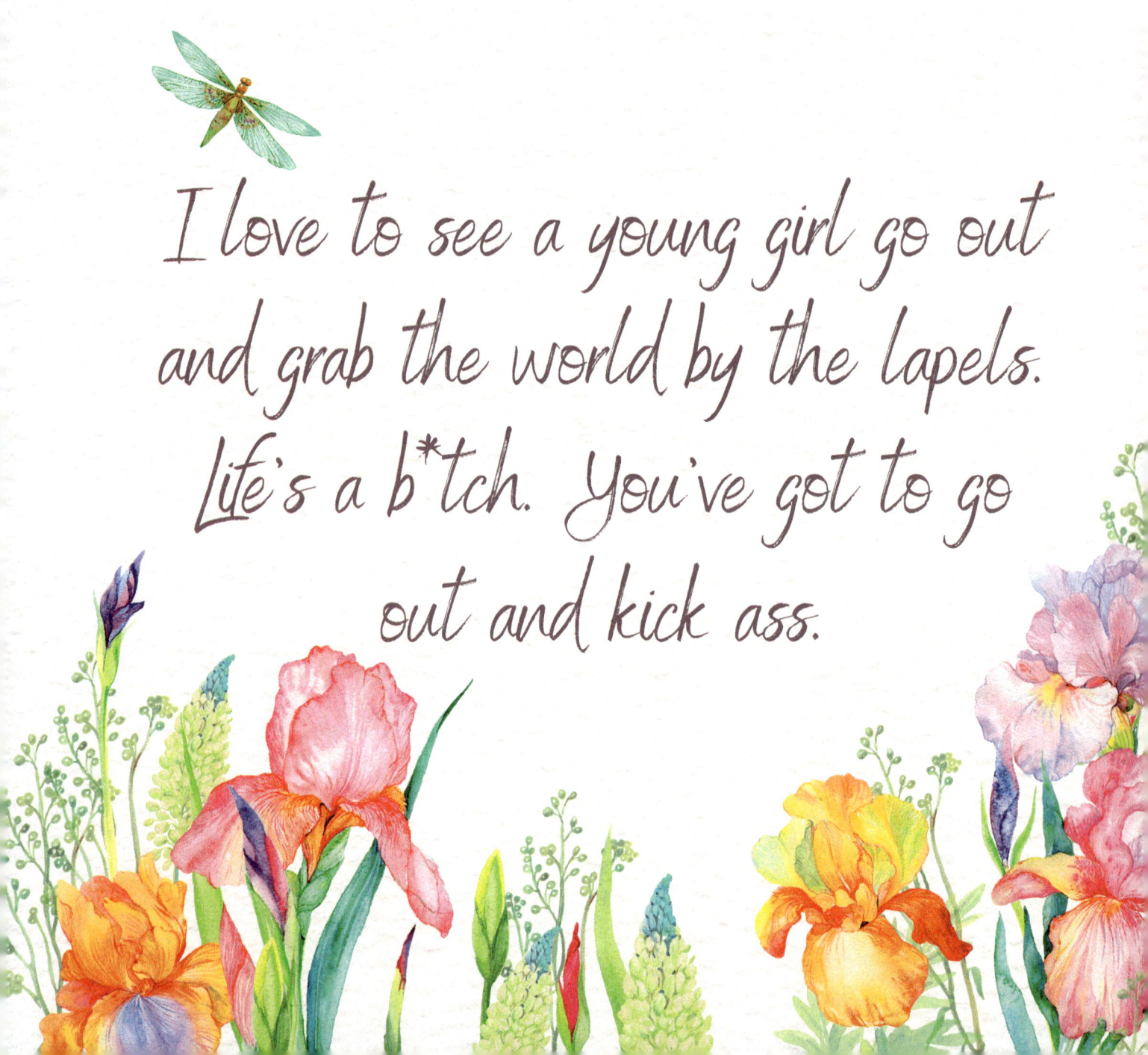

I love to see a young girl go out and grab the world by the lapels. Life's a b*tch. You've got to go out and kick ass.

JANE GOODALL

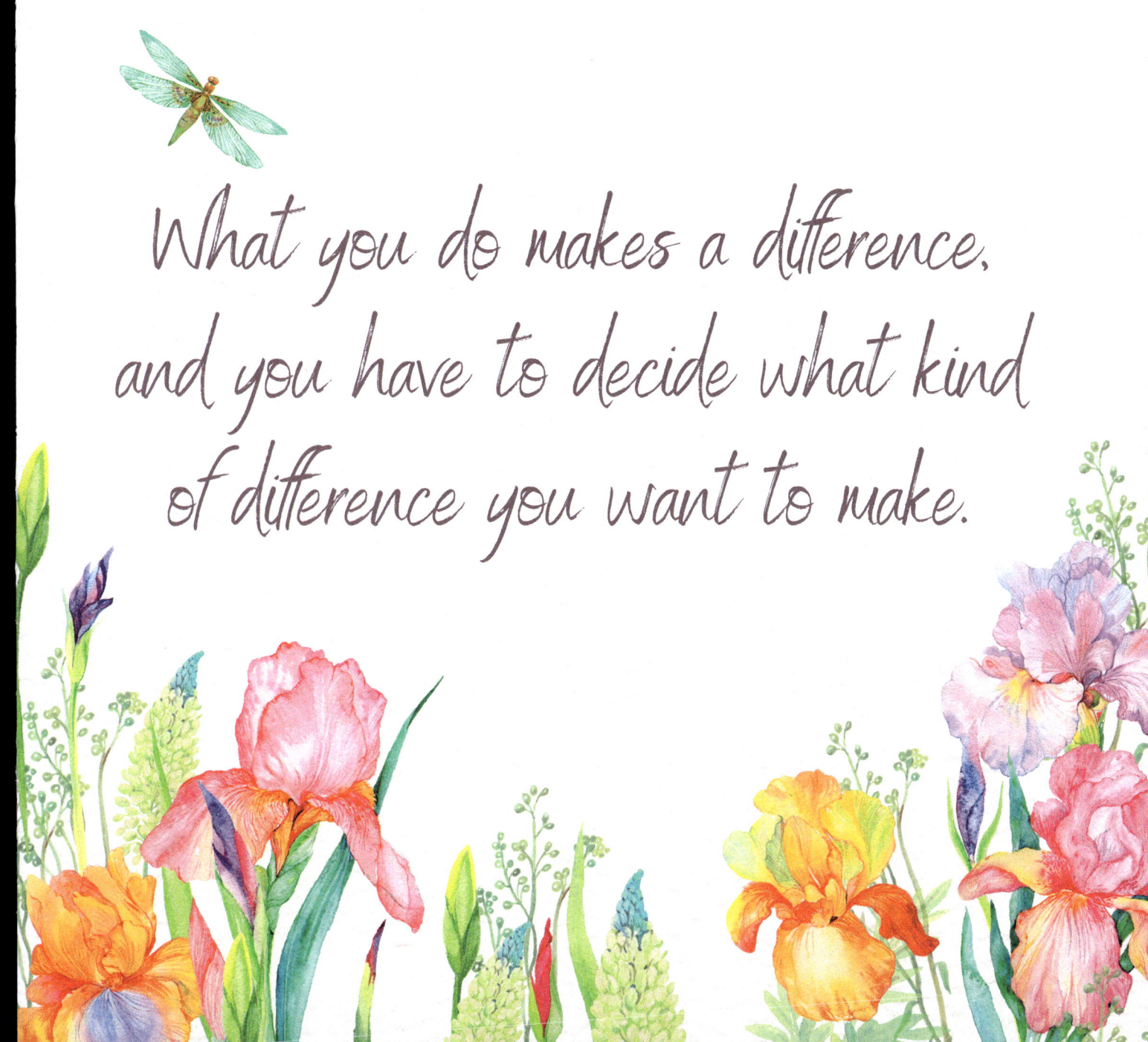

What you do makes a difference, and you have to decide what kind of difference you want to make.

LOUISE HAY

I choose to make the rest of my life the best of my life.

ALICE WALKER

The most common way people give up their power is by thinking they don't have any.

LEYMAH GBOWEE

You can never leave footprints that last if you are always walking on tiptoe.

ELEANOR ROOSEVELT

The future belongs to those who believe in the beauty of their dreams.

SHONDA RHIMES

You can waste your lives drawing lines. Or you can live your life crossing them.

OPRAH WINFREY

The biggest adventure you can take is to live the life of your dreams.

MARIE CURIE

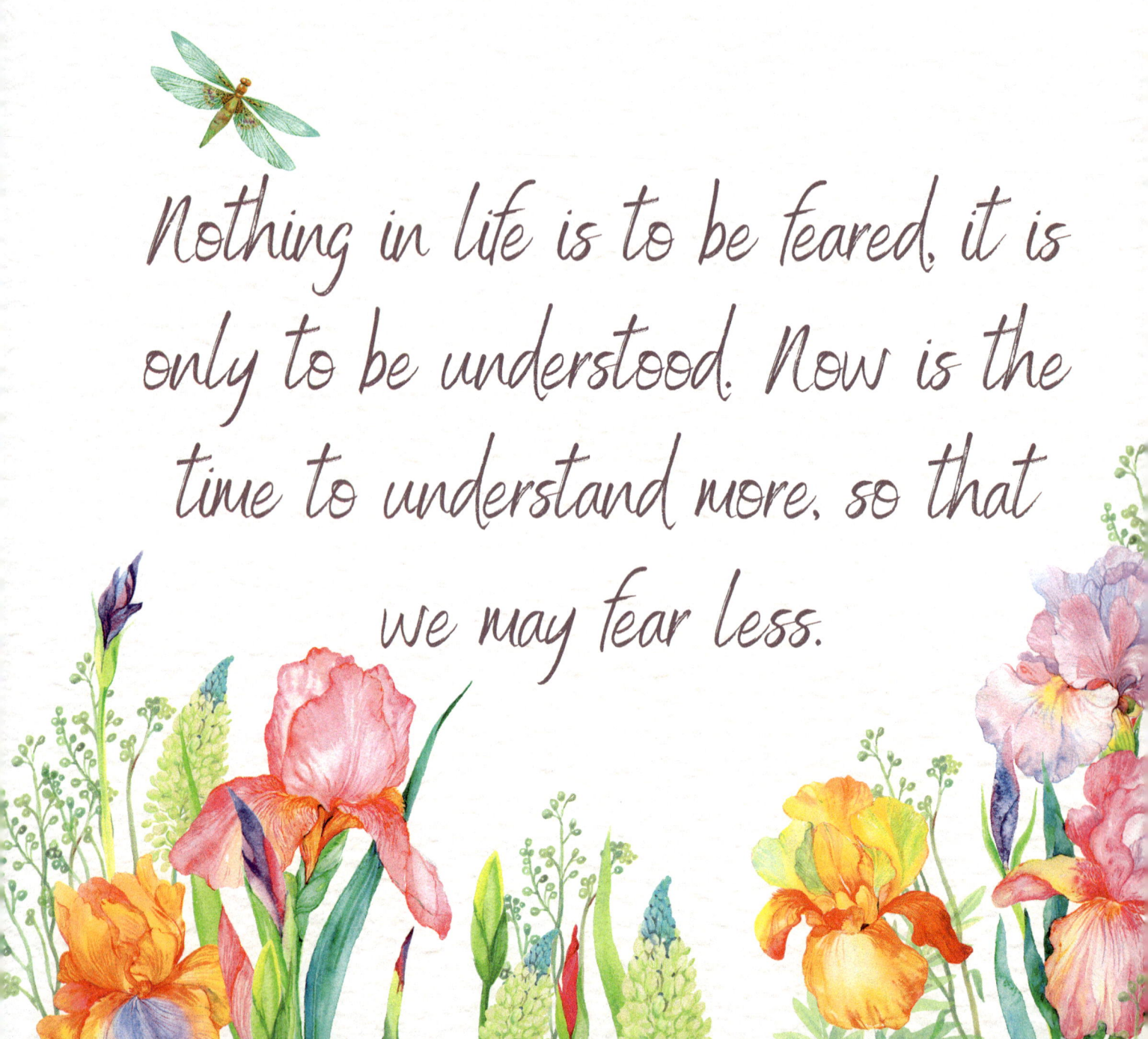

Nothing in life is to be feared, it is only to be understood. Now is the time to understand more, so that we may fear less.

RUTH BADER GINSBURG

Fight for the things that you care about, but do it in a way that will lead others to join you.

FRIDA KAHLO

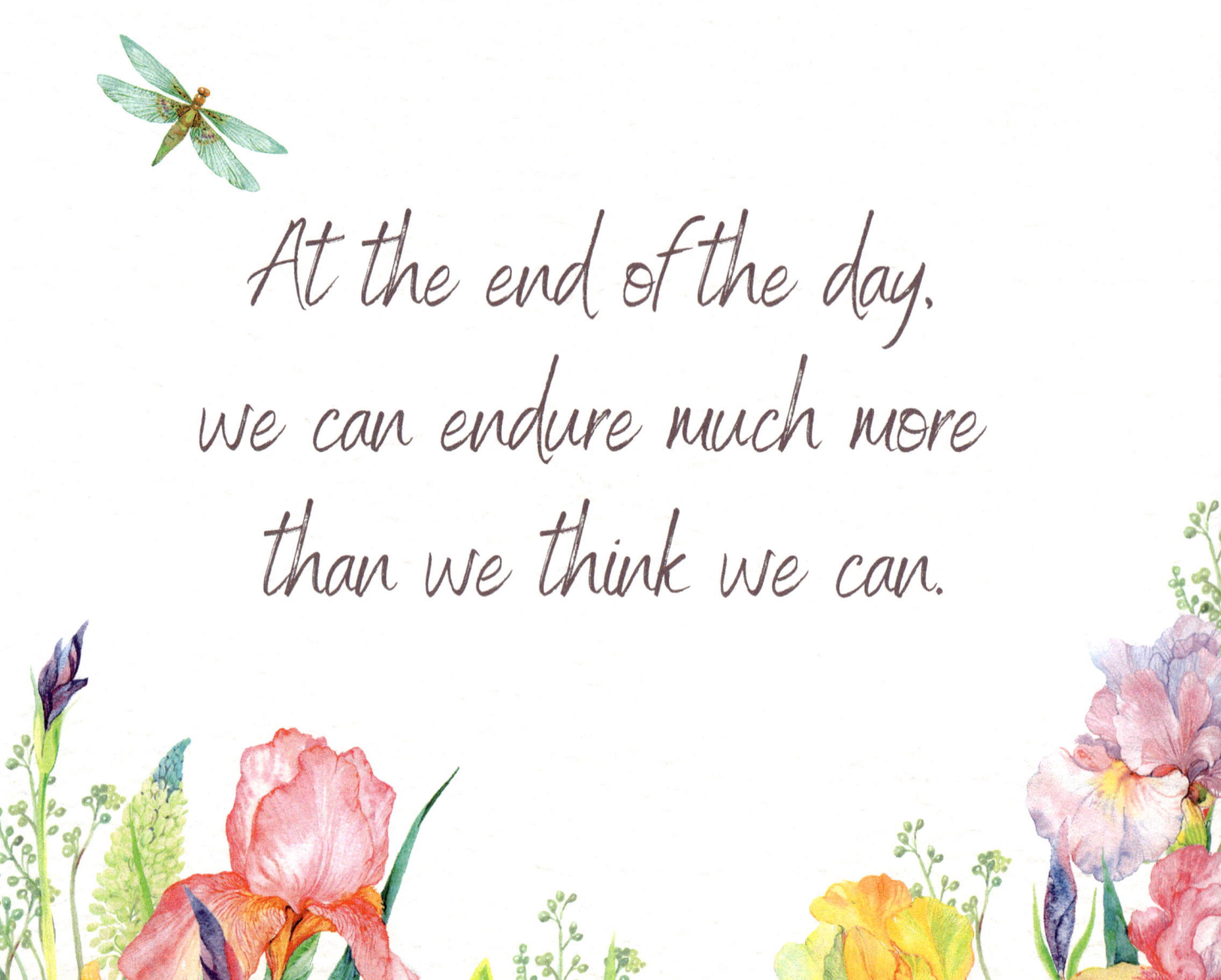

At the end of the day, we can endure much more than we think we can.

MICHELLE OBAMA

When they go low, we go high.

AUDREY HEPBURN

The best thing to hold onto in life is each other.

INDIRA GANDHI

There are two kinds of people, those who do the work and those who take the credit. Try to be in the first group; there is less competition there.

AUNG SAN SUU KYI

The only real prison is fear, and the only real freedom is freedom from fear.

SUSAN SONTAG

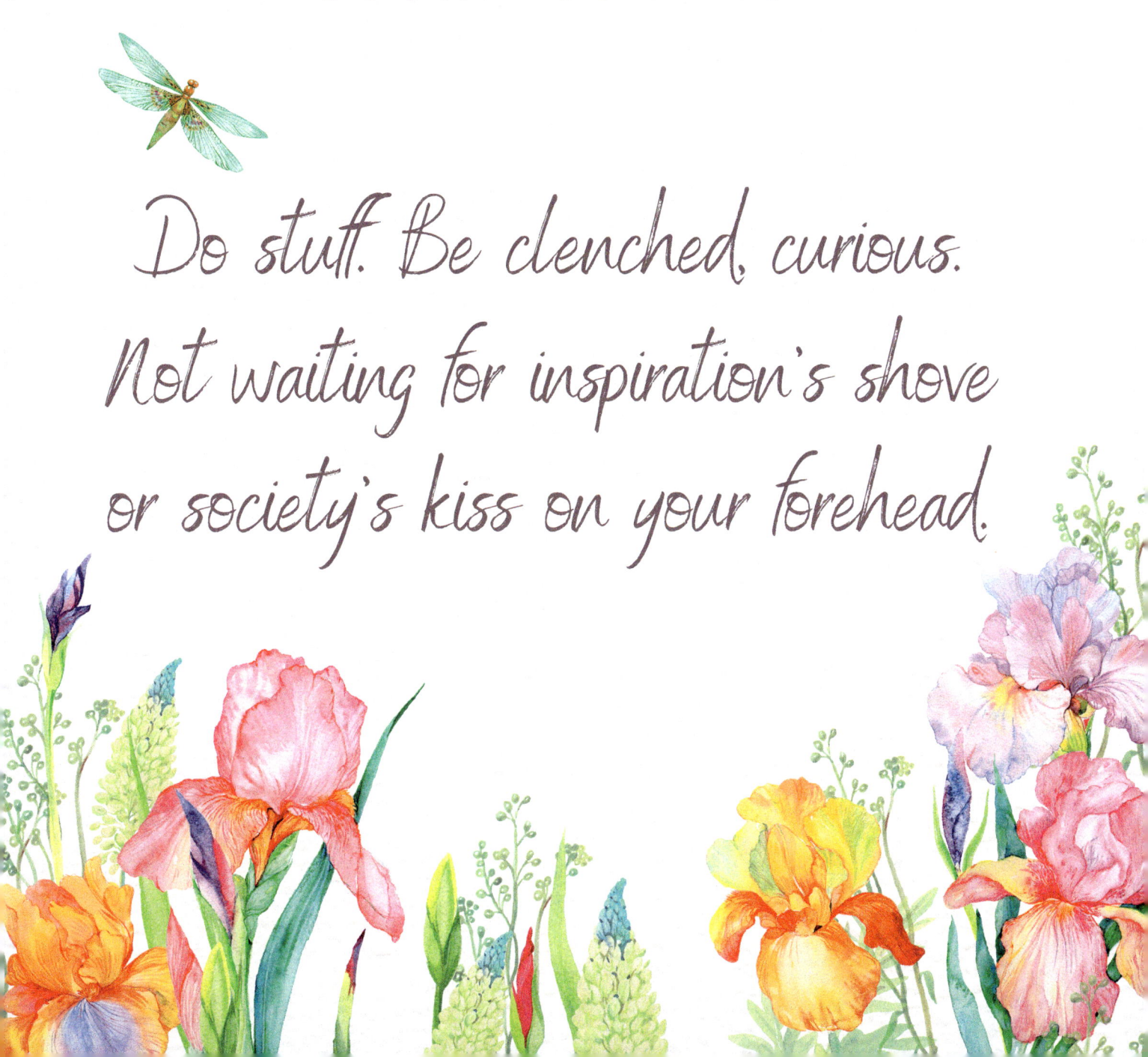

Do stuff. Be clenched, curious. Not waiting for inspiration's shove or society's kiss on your forehead.

SOJOURNER TRUTH

If women want any rights more than they's got, why don't they just take them, and not be talking about it.

ELEANOR ROOSEVELT

You must do the things you think you cannot do.

HARRIET TUBMAN

Every great dream begins with a dreamer. You have within you the strength, the patience, and the passion to reach for the stars to change the world.

RUPI KAUR

You are your own soulmate.

BILLIE JEAN KING

Champions keep playing until they get it right.

MADELEINE ALBRIGHT

There is a special place in hell for women who don't help other women.

GLORIA STEINEM

A feminist is anyone who recognizes the equality and full humanity of women and men.

LUCILLE BALL

Love yourself first and everything else falls into line.

BRENE BROWN

Vulnerability is not winning or losing; it's having the courage to show up and be seen when we have no control over the outcome.

MOTHER TERESA

Spread love everywhere you go. Let no one ever come to you without leaving happier.

ANGELA MERKEL

When it comes to human dignity, we cannot make compromises.

AMELIA EARHART

The most effective way to do it, is to do it.

MARIE CURIE

We must have perseverance and above all confidence in ourselves. We must believe that we are gifted for something.

AUDREY HEPBURN

Nothing is impossible, the word itself says 'I'm possible!'

J.K. ROWLING

It is our choices that show what we truly are, far more than our abilities.

TONI MORRISON

If you want to fly, you have to give up the things that weigh you down.

ROSA PARKS

You must never be fearful about what you are doing when it is right.

SUSAN B. ANTHONY

Failure is impossible.

JANE AUSTEN

I hate to hear you talk about all women as if they were fine ladies instead of rational creatures.

MALALA YOUSAFZAI

One book, one pen, one child, and one teacher can change the world.

COCO CHANEL

Success is often achieved by those who don't know that failure is inevitable.

MAYA ANGELOU

I've learned that people will forget what you said, people will forget what you did, but people will never forget how you made them feel.

MARGARET THATCHER

If you want something said, ask a man; if you want something done, ask a woman.

MOTHER TERESA

Not all of us can do great things. But we can do small things with great love.

LOUISA MAY ALCOTT

I am not afraid of storms for I am learning how to sail my ship.

HELEN KELLER

Alone we can do so little; together we can do so much.

ANNE FRANK

Despite everything, I believe that people are really good at heart.

SYLVIA PLATH

I took a deep breath and listened to the old bray of my heart. I am. I am. I am.

ROSA PARKS

Stand for something or you will fall for anything.

ELIZABETH GILBERT

Embrace the glorious mess that you are.

AMELIA EARHART

The most difficult thing is the decision to act, the rest is merely tenacity.

EMMA WATSON

Feminism is about giving women choice. Feminism is not a stick with which to beat other women with.

OPRAH WINFREY

Turn your wounds into wisdom.

SIMONE DE BEAUVOIR

One is not born, but rather becomes, a woman.

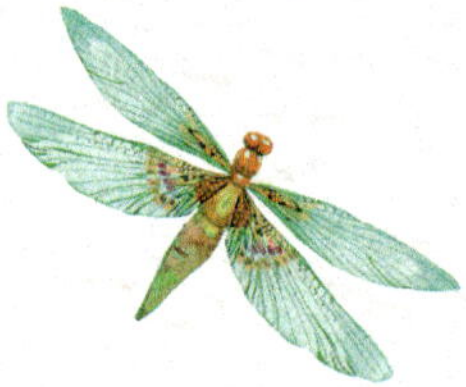

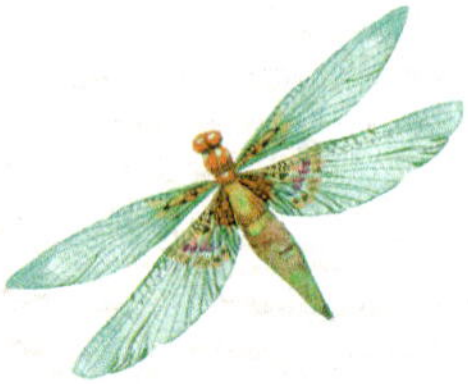

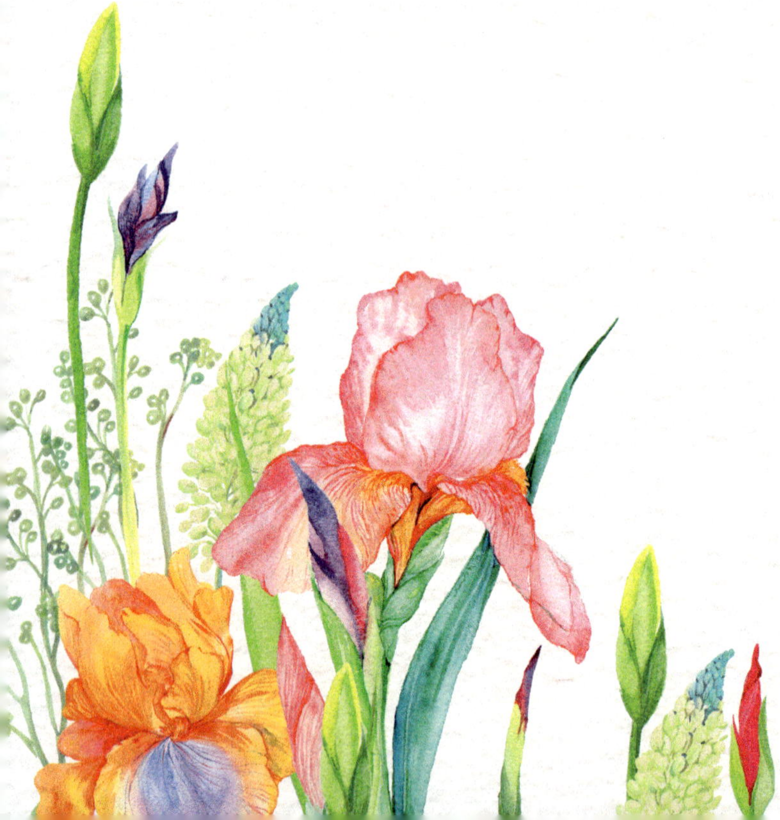

Printed in Great Britain
by Amazon